The Things My Grandmother

Used to Say

The Things My Grandmother Used to Say

Used to Say

Lessons Learned
by
Listening to Words of Wisdom

Published by Truth Publications, LLC
www.truth-brand.com

The Things That My Grandmother Used to Say:
Lessons Learned by Listening to Words of Wisdom
ISBN: 979-8-9890909-1-4
Copyright ©2024 by Veronica Smith-Creer
www.mayor-sunshine.com

Table of Contents

Dedication

I would like to dedicate this book to my mother, Alberta Lynell Brock Smith. She was born Bertha Mae Brock, but legally changed her name. I watched my mother change things throughout her lifetime. I am dedicating this book to her, knowing that she and her mother had the most beautiful bond, the kind of bond she recreated with her own daughters. My mother was like my grandmother in so many ways, even though they led different kinds of lives. I am grateful for the example my mother showed us of being a loving daughter, a supportive sister, a true helpmate of a wife, and a nurturing mother. She was able to be an amazing "Nana" to her grandchildren. I always say I hope I made her proud before she transitioned and that I would be making her proud now. I listened to you, Momma! Thank you for everything you did and everything you said.

Introduction

My maternal grandmother was Eva Mary Polly Louise McKelphin Brock, born to Angelyn and Cullen McKelphin. She gave birth to 12 children, none of which being multiple births, with her husband Jerome "Jep" Brock. My mother, Alberta Lynell Brock Smith, was their third child, and only the second to live passed being a newborn. Two children did not live past birth. Ironically, the first four were girls. My grandparents had six girls and six boys, with four girls and six boys growing into adulthood--12 children in the span of about 18 years! By the time the youngest child was born, the oldest children were married with children of their own while the youngest were still in school and at home.

My grandmother had a close relationship with all her children despite the range in ages. Of course, the relationships were different, but close nonetheless. She lived in a small town named Pearl River very close to Slidell, LA, by the time I was born. Her home was small, but very tidy. Her home was between her sister and her niece's homes. I remember the walls were covered with pictures of family, both young and old.

Grandmother loved her grandchildren! We, my siblings and I, were her only Arkansas grandchildren. Most of my first cousins lived in New Orleans, LA. That was usually our destination when we would visit her. Her grandchildren there called her Maw Maw (sounds like Mo Mo). Our oldest cousin there called her Momma. Over the years, she went from Grandma Eva, Maw Maw, Maw Maw Eva to Mama Eva. We were all her babies, and we all thought we were her favorite.

I have always been told that I look like her. It is one of the greatest compliments I could ever be paid! She was beautiful with long hair and a sassy attitude. I am referred to as Little Eva by some of my relatives, and I absolutely love it! As a grandmother, she kept us all in line, but I can never recall her spanking any of us or even raising her voice.

Her appearance, as beautiful as she was, did not hold a candle to her spirit or energy. It filled the room, and her voice was unmistakable! Mama Eva had a laugh that ended with a wide smile that showed off her teeth with a few trimmed in gold. There was no one like her, and we knew it!

Every year, our family would go visit our grandmother in Pearl River, LA, sometimes several times a year. One of the things I always loved about the visits was listening to her speak. She had a Louisiana dialect, and I am not sure what her accent really was, considering she had lived in Mississippi as well all those years when she was married. I do know that she said things differently from the way we did and some of her words were, let's say, her very own, or so we thought. "Betwixt" was a word we had never heard, but "betwixt and between" was a phrase she used from time to time.

There were so many things she would say that made us as children laugh. The way she could turn a phrase to prove a point or teach a lesson was uncanny. I did not know my grandmother's mother, but her name was Angelyn, shortened to Angie. My mother often spoke about her, calling her

Grandma Angie. I saw pictures of her in my grandmother's house. She was beautiful and from her appearance I could see the traces of Indian descent I was told she possessed. I wondered at times if my grandmother got any of her sayings from her mother.

By the time our mother was an adult and married, her parents were divorced. I never knew my maternal grandparents as a married couple. My grandmother never spoke ill of our grandfather in our presence, but somehow, I knew not to ask too many questions about him when she was around. He, on the other hand, would always tell me, Little Eva, to tell my grandmother to come home to him. I would tell her, and she would laugh. I never questioned why they weren't together. I never asked him why she wasn't there with him, and, somehow, I knew not to ask her. I guess, because she would laugh, it never crossed my mind that she could have left him, that she didn't like him, or that he was mean to her. I would later find out the truth. She did leave him and although I think she loved him, she couldn't have liked him very much. He was more than mean to her, he was abusive.

From the stories I have been told, the home life in my grandparents' home was not the best. My grandfather was as good-looking as my grandmother was beautiful. The fact that he had a child out of wedlock while he was married to my grandmother says she was forgiving. The child was my Uncle Julius, who was around the same age as their first child together, my Aunt Bessie. The fact that she stayed proves that she either believed he would never be unfaithful again, or she would deal with it. She went on to have 11 more children with him and stayed about 30 more years.

My grandfather was a hard man by his children's account. I did not know him to be *that* man. His children picked cotton, worked the fields, tended animals, and kept the house clean. My mother and aunts were not exempt from the field work and did housework also. His parents were Percy and George Brock. My great grandfather, George Brock, was half white. By complexion, my great grandmother was very dark skinned and probably 100% black. My aunts and uncles are just about every complexion from light skinned with the oldest girls, to very dark skinned with the baby boy. My grandfather did not let that variation in complexity rule the way he treated them. He was hard on them all!

I have no idea about my grandparents' home life. They both came from large families, and that was pretty much the way of life with their generation. Lots of children meant lots of work could get done! I can remember meeting many of my mother's aunts and uncles on both sides, and I detected a closeness. There just wasn't enough information from anyone for me to determine what growing up was like for them. I can only assume with the time and the circumstances, things at home were hard, and each child was eager to leave to find his or her own place in life.

I was in my 20's when my grandmother passed away from a massive heart attack at the age of 86 years old. We think it was because she was working so hard after her home had flooded. No one has ever mentioned any health issues that she might have been dealing with at the time. I knew she was very independent even at her age. Having been a single woman for quite some time at that point, she didn't ask anyone to do much for her if she could do it herself. She was doing a lot of physical labor to get things in order. That meant a lot of hours throwing things away that she loved and doing it in a home she may never live in again. In retrospect, I think she may have been saying goodbye to her home and to her life as she looked for the last time at her belongings that had been damaged. One last look before she went home. She would never finish cleaning or get to live in her home again.

I knew that my grandmother's family lived in the homes around hers. When I was a child, I would not have thought they were related. Aunt Margaret did not look anything like her to me. She was older, and while my grandmother was lighter skinned, Aunt Margaret was darker. Aunt Margaret's daughter, Lillie, looked more like my grandmother. It is amazing what we don't understand as children, but it makes so much more sense when we are older. We all look like someone in our families, I suppose. My grandmother and her sisters may not have looked much alike to me as child, but maybe they did resemble each other more if I had known how to look at them. From conversations, not actual pictures that I can recall, there were more sisters and brothers. Now I wish I had more conversations and even looked at more pictures to ask some questions.

My grandmother never said much about her family members, even though they were right there. Even when she would visit, we didn't talk about her siblings or her life as a girl. She never spoke about her life at home with her parents. She never spoke about her mother or her father. It seemed that her mother, Angie, was a sweet woman, but I got that idea more from my mother than her mother. Not much was ever said about her father. Speaking of her sisters did give us one story of a sister that went to jail for killing a white man who was taking advantage of her. She went to jail for the crime, of course, but the story always gave me a sense of pride. I came from women who did not allow anyone for any reason to think stepping over a boundary would end up in their favor.

My grandmother was strength to me. As a single woman she did what she wanted, when she wanted, and how she wanted. I could not imagine her being dependent on anyone. She didn't have a husband, but she didn't want for anything. She spoke with pride when she shared her words of wisdom.

My mother looked up to her even in her adulthood. She seemed to be in awe of her when I was a child. Grandma Eva, I would find out later in my life, walked through hell and was not burned!

When we get together to talk about her, everyone has a favorite story. One thing we can all agree on is that she taught us lessons with the words she spoke and the life she lived. She had a way of making every conversation with her feel like a therapy session once it was over. Little phrases that seemed strange when we were younger took shape in our later years. Our beloved grandmother passed away in 1995, but her legacy, life, and love live on in "the things our grandma used to say"!

Chapter One

You're Living Your
Best Days in Your Parents' House

I still can remember the day as if it were yesterday! Grandma was visiting our home after I had graduated from high school. I was still living at home with my parents, but I was working and going to school at our local community college. Somehow, she and I started a conversation about my moving out of their house and finding an apartment. I remember telling her that it was time for me to be on my own. She was so sweet in her response, but it was very much on point. After listening to all my little issues and problems, my grandmother simply said, "You are living your best days in your parents' house."

She listened as I spoke about wanting to come and go like a grown-up. My parents had a curfew, even though I was by all accounts "grown." I mentioned that I had just received a credit card in my name, and I was working multiple jobs and could pay my own bills. I was tired of living with my mother and father. I definitely was tired of their telling me what I could and could not do while I lived there. Shouldn't I be living an independent life like her?

My grandmother listened so intently, keeping eye contact as I described how my life would be when I could move out and be on my own. I was waiting for her to respond that she agreed and that I should move forward with moving out and being independent like her. Instead, I received, "You are living your best life in your parents' house." Oh, there was more, but that was definitely the theme of her answer! She went on to say that the utility bills were paid already. My mother cooked every day, so food was not an issue. The laundry was done already whether I did it or not. She did the whole pros and cons of my moving out and ended up with, "You are living your best days in your parents' house."

I did not ask her how she knew. I had no knowledge of her childhood. I knew nothing concerning how she grew up and how things were for her or family life with her parents or siblings. I have never heard anything about any of that, yet there was no need to question her, since what she said was unfortunately right on point. Many of us think that we are invincible in our 20's. We have everything under control, and our plans are perfect! My grandmother broke things down in such a way that an argument was a no go. After she finished, I almost cried. How had I overlooked all the things she mentioned? She never said, "I know from experience"; she never said, "My children will agree"; she never even said, "Do as I say, not as I have done." Her explanation hit home in such a way that I stayed home an entire year after she passed away. Those years were truly my best!

The advice she gave to me is the same advice I have found myself giving to others. Sometimes we get in a hurry. It's a sure sign of youth. We think we have it all figured out without even really having a clue. Youth gives you the fallacy of being invincible. In my 20's, I was so ready to step out and create a laundry list of bills that I hadn't taken the time actually to count the cost. Like most people at that age, I was looking for a life, for a freedom that possibly would never exist. I would be confining myself to a different kind of dependency and, more than likely, debt. I am so glad I listened to what my grandmother was saying and understood what she meant.

Not everyone may have the same situation that I lived in at the time of our discussion. My grandmother read mine perfectly, though! Ultimately, the whole concept is to count the cost of every move you make. It's not enough to go from your emotions and definitely not enough to go from your imagination! What my grandmother was telling me was to recognize where I was, what I wanted, and when to make the move that would be beneficial and make the most sense for me. She analyzed my situation from what she knew to be true. How much sense would it make for me to leave my parents' home for the reasons I had stated, only to have to come back or to need them to help me financially?

The conversation and the situation taught me more than I had anticipated. The concept of living your best life transcends much more than my living in my parents' house. It applies to relationships, jobs, and opportunities. That conversation taught me to count the cost in all the decisions I have made since then. When you count the cost of any situation, you can determine whether these truly are your best days or if better days are coming!

The concept of thinking things through and counting all the costs helped me when I ultimately found myself in a position of leadership. Advice is not always asked for, but when you observe individuals on a daily basis, you are able to find ways to share your own life experiences and to answer those questions never spoken. For example, when I had the privilege of serving as mayor of my hometown, I was able to speak from a platform much larger than before and to be transparent about my life's lessons. Your parents' home can be used as a metaphor as your place of comfort, security, and preparation for the world. I am appreciative to have had that place.

Take the time truly to listen to these invaluable conversations. As a current "Mimi," since I wasn't ready to be a grandmother, I am always attempting to pour knowledge into young people. I pray the words of my ancestors continue to speak truth into the next generations. My children have profited from those words and the actions they evoked. Can you recognize your best days?

Chapter Two

If You Play With A Puppy,
It Will Lick You In The Mouth

We never had a dog. There were five children in our family, and none of us liked dogs. I can remember my dad talking about dogs, but not my mom. Neither one of my parents was scared of them, but it was a different story with us children. I can say that growing up, I never really liked them. I was scared of them for the most part, for whatever reason. I can remember us dog sitting for one of my siblings' friends once. It was a learning experience!

My grandmother may have had a dog. I'm not sure that she did, but I do remember dogs being in the little community in which she and her sisters lived. I don't remember her playing with dogs at all. When I was growing up, it was not a part of our culture to have dogs in the house as we see so frequently now. If you possessed a dog, it was kept outside. If you were fancy, it had an actual doghouse! We didn't know very many fancy people.

My grandmother spent time with all her children, which meant she spent lots of time with her grandchildren. I think we all anxiously awaited our turn each year. Since she lived closer to New Orleans, our cousins who lived there got to see her the most. We were the only ones in Arkansas. Our time with her was precious! It was also filled with great conversations.

Mama Eva was observant. She was very vocal about her thoughts concerning what she observed. Thinking back on so many memories, I hear her voice clearly. She watched our interactions with our parents and with our siblings. She lived to see many of us get jobs and go into the workforce. She attended several weddings and watched us begin our own families. She had a front-row seat to the good, the bad, and the ugly! Her background might have been hard, but she was determined to use it to make ours better!

When she said, "If you play with a puppy, it will lick you in the mouth" it made me wonder, "Why puppies, Grandma?" It makes me laugh and smile really big as she would. But there was a seriousness in this warning. It wasn't playful puppies rolling around the floor. It wasn't an act of playing at all. How were we to understand this warning while we were children? I'm not sure she expected us to get it fully at the time, but the delivery was what mattered. She said it in context to make sure we heard the words and placed them in the correct connotation for the situation. It was always caution that what might seem harmless, could lead to something very different.

You see, playing with a puppy can be fun! What is your visual when you think about playing with a puppy? More than likely, you see a furry, adorable puppy running and rolling around on the floor or in a yard. You see the cuteness of the puppy's energy as it runs around. You probably can hear in your imagination the barks and baby growls. You envision the puppy rolling around with a ball or a chew toy or even nestled in the arms of a child or an adult. The picture you envision is one of welcomed cuteness instead of the warning of caution, I'm sure.

Now consider the fact that not everyone thinks a puppy licking you in the mouth is cute. May I remind you that the culture that we are experiencing now with dogs is not the same culture of my grandmother's time. It's not the same culture that I grew up in at all! A puppy licking you in the mouth was degrading! It was embarrassing, and it was nasty! My grandmother's analogy was the progression of something starting off fun, even cute, but ending up with you in a compromising situation.

She rarely liked my boyfriends. I was always afraid for her to meet them. She would always be nice, but she would always give me her honest opinion about them. Every single time she was absolutely correct! On one occasion, I remember very distinctly being upset about her commentary. I had been dating this particular guy for a few months. He was good-looking and by all accounts very popular. I thought he was a catch! I was in high school, so I was almost a grown-up. He just might be my husband! Or so I thought. He was fairly well liked by my family.

Well, I introduced him to my grandmother, and she was nice. After he left, I got the real deal! She admitted he was cute, but to her, he was a puppy! She broke my heart explaining that he was just fun. He would not be serious about me, and my thinking he was more than a temporary factor in my life would not turn out to be a pretty situation. I was mad! How could she say all of that from one encounter? Did I mention she was never wrong? Her words have never left me. What is cute for you right now can come back and make you look foolish. I watched him prove her words to be true.

It's not just relationships of the opposite sex. It's not just relationships at all. Be careful what you allow yourself to get comfortable with from other people or situations. Some things may start off harmlessly. You may not see the potential danger. Be cautious about playing with puppies. It can change very quickly from laughter to embarrassment.

I saw the same situations play out in people that turned out to be "puppies" in my life. The spirit of discernment allowed me to see some things, but I must admit that I played with some of them. It left me seeing her analogy playing out in a very public way at times. What was perceived as good advice from what I considered to be good friends, turned out to be some of them "licking me in the mouth!"

Being the mayor of a first-class city was very public! There were many times when what started out as fun or even a friendship took a very wrong turn. I had to learn to recognize the long-term effects of short-term decisions. I could not take some of the individuals that I had once called "friends" at face value, or discern them by the things I knew of them in the past. My grandmother's advice served me well in my position, and I am grateful. I still deal with some of the "puppies." I have learned to keep them at a distance.

Chapter Three

A Cow Needs Its Tail More Than One Summer

I never saw my grandmother around a cow. In the cul-de-sac where she lived, the only animals were dogs and occasional cats. Now my grandfather, her ex-husband, had cows! My grandparents' relationship was very strange to me as a child. While I knew she was my mother's mother and he was my mother's father, I never knew them as a married couple and rarely ever saw them together. I am not sure why this analogy never seemed strange for me to hear from her instead of him. For whatever reason, it didn't.

My grandmother had a way with people. She was always very friendly and had such a beautiful smile! Her laugh was genuine, and her eyes were happy. Her personality seemed to draw people to her. She called most people "baby." I couldn't imagine anyone not liking her. I couldn't imagine anyone not loving her.

My grandmother lived in an era not far removed from slavery. She had a front-row seat to people being treated badly simply for the color of their skin. Having the same skin didn't keep someone from being harmed either. As a matter of fact, I would learn later in my life that my grandmother had taken some major blows from people close enough to land them in painful places. I couldn't tell that she was ever bitter about those things. My image of her was that of a strong, yet nurturing woman.

One of the things, I believe, that kept her balanced is this saying: "A cow needs its tail more than one summer." Oh, it baffled me at the time like the rest of them, but I grew to understand it better in time. The way she put things together would soon make more sense to me. To be honest, initially I didn't even understand the cow's need for a tail at all! It was explained that the cow uses its tail to swat the flies away from its backside when they were very prevalent in the summertime.

I considered myself a good friend. I didn't have a ton of friends, but I had a few growing up. There were times when I shared with her about friends turning out to be less than what I felt I was to them. I wanted to be treated by them the way I treated them. With that expectation not always being the case with high school girls, I eventually found out you don't always get what you give! Somehow you are not needed.

Well, whether you can recall your high school years or not, there are always relationships in which the people who have taken advantage of your kindness, or your competence, or your position, find themselves in need of it again! People sometimes get the notion that they have gotten all that they wanted from you once you recognize they mean no good-- almost to the point of being upset with you that you found out about their motives or intentions!

Let's go back to the cow's tail. We can agree that seasons, for the most part, bring about the same situations every year. Needing a tail in the summertime is a given because flies will be prominent every summer! How could the cow survive without her tail any summer when flies show up every summer? Keeping that fact in perspective, I came to realize that most people, in general, didn't realize that what I brought to the table was much like a cow's tail. It was a necessity! You will need me again, just as you needed me the last time.

I don't consider myself arrogant by understanding my worth. I think through everything my grandmother encountered and even lived through and realize, it made her understand her worth. The tail of a cow is one its smallest features, but it is needed in a major way! It gave the cow relief from the flies and even some comfort. I am sure that the cow doesn't take it for granted.

Don't let anyone make you feel insignificant, especially when you realize what you bring to the table. It may seem small and even effortless to you. It may be as natural as the swinging of a cow's tail, but it is needed! What would life be like for the cow without its tail? I am sure the cow does not want to know.

Although they may not know it, or they may not want you to know that they do, people understand what you bring to the table, to the situation, to the organization, to the company, or to the city. They would like you to think that it is insignificant, and that others can do without it--that *they* can do without it. Some who have been thus dismayed have used the phrase, "You will need me again," but I think my grandmother said it best when she declared, "A cow needs its tail more than one summer!"

I feel as though my gift of gab, my love of speaking, has been a blessing to others. God blessed me with this gift to share information, to motivate others, and to provide inspiration. As a mayor, I used it for all those things. I was transparent as a city official, and while some people didn't want to know everything, it was a part of "my ministry." It seemed insignificant to some, but I'm reminded that many may believe that ignorance is bliss. Others, for whatever reason, hated my gift of gab and the transparent sharing of information, and they made no secret of it. Transparency and the truth are not always welcomed and can even be threatening to those who profit from secrecy and lies. I didn't stop my transparent communication, because it was, again, a ministry to me, and needed.

I am no longer a mayor, but I am still the same person I was when I sat in that chair in that office in that building. My information, my gift of gab, is missing now. I still get calls and questions from the public because they miss being told what is going on in our city. I guess my grandmother would say, "They are missing that cow's tail!"

The perfect way for your gift to be appreciated is for it to be absent. This information goes for everyone, because while we need to understand the value of what we possess, it is also important to believe that other people have their own value as well. Recognize the cow's tail in everyone and don't wait until you need it to acknowledge it. Summers are lasting longer these days, and they are filled with flies, if you know what I mean!

Chapter Four

If You Dig In Trash, It Will Get In Your Eyes

My grandmother wore glasses. She wore them through many style changes. I saw pictures of her in the old cat-eyed glasses with the black frames. She was a much younger woman then. I never liked those, but they were so pretty on her. I did get to witness a few of the different frames she wore that had much bigger lenses. She wore them all well! I may be a bit biased, though.

One thing I do remember is that she rarely had her glasses off her face. It was almost strange for me to see her with them off. The only time she wasn't wearing them was while she slept. Putting them on first thing in the morning was her tradition. She needed to see.

As I write and remember, I understand her vision much better than I did as a child. I do realize that I knew even back then that glasses help you see better, but that is only in the physical sense. This saying is less about what you can see with your eyes and more about what "vision" is beyond your sight!

We get caught up in people, in material things, and money. Sometimes that leads to things beyond what we can see with our physical eyes. Fun people who like to have a good time and party don't start off looking like trash. Having nice cars, fancy clothes, and a nice house doesn't look like trash in the beginning. Lots of money and disposable cash doesn't look anything like trash to us. Those all seem like good things! Don't they?

As stated before in a previous chapter, my grandmother shared her opinions. She was never nasty to people in general and never to our friends specifically. You didn't always have to ask for her to share her opinions, and although you may not always like them, they were never harsh. She knew how to read people, and it didn't take her long. Can I say she knew trash when she saw it?

Her relationship with her children was a bit colorful! I was a young adult when my grandmother passed away, but my childhood was filled with memories of how she handled her children. She had a different approach to her daughters from the one she used with her sons. Nurturing to all of them, she had almost a pity for her sons. She was still "mothering" them when they all had families of their own. She saw something that I could not see, and I wish I had understood more back then so that I really could have asked her about her vision.

There was a time when all her sons were doing well. They had nice homes and cars as well as nice jobs. They all had beautiful wives and children! Unfortunately, she saw trash get in their eyes. Please don't judge them too harshly since you've probably gotten trash in your eyes, too!

My grandmother's analogy was simply that you can get so deep into something that it can change your outlook on life. It can change the way you see things. Digging in trash for many of us is staying too long in a bad situation that started off as a good one. When you think about it, most trash starts off as something you wanted until it became useless, used up, broken, or replaced. Now think about the things you once treasured that became trash.

You also must see that the analogy points to things that were never good for you in the first place, and they captured your sight. For some it might be drinking. It starts off very harmlessly and may just be a social thing. It might be something you use to take the edge off every now and then. It may be a relationship that starts off innocently like a friendship or work relationship. It could be something you watch on the internet from time to time to take you to another place for a while. All these things can end up being trash. The way you delve deeper into any of them is just as powerful as digging in a garbage can. While the stench of garbage literally can get in your eyes, digging deep into any of these activities will cloud your vision of your reality. You will think that no one can see you in the trash can. It has destroyed your vision.

Grandmother cautioned her children, her grandchildren, and anyone that would listen that some situations would end up being trash in your life and ultimately get in your eyes. She saw it happen even when she advised against it. The things you think you can't live without, the trash that will become your reality if you make the choice to immerse yourself in it will change your view of yourself and life in general.

It was sad to watch at times how her heart seemed to break when she couldn't change the choices made by those she loved. I realize now as a woman, as a wife, as a mother, as a "Mimi," as a friend and role model, that it is easy to recognize, but hard to watch, someone close to you decide to dig in the trash of life. I found a new respect for her when I found out how in so many ways, she escaped what was turning into trash to keep it from getting in her eyes. She wanted the same clear vision for her loved ones.

I wish I could say that my vision has always been 20/20. There were times when I could distinctly see that I was going headfirst into the dumpster with some situations in life. It's a humbling situation to have to step back and see what you were heading into without actually seeing it. As a mayor, I was unfortunately surrounded by trash. Some of it was mistaken friendships that turned out to be gutter rats. At times, it was the accolades of so-called supporters who turned out to be snakes. It was even those who vowed to work with me that turned out to be the very ones working against me. I'm grateful that my vision may have been distorted for a time, but like my grandmother, I was able to put on my glasses! I'm grateful that I was able to see before the trash could get in my eyes. To protect your VISION, WATCH what you dig in!

Chapter Five

It's Not What You Do, But How You Do It!

This was one of my all-time favorite sayings of my grandmother! Oh, the look on her face when she would utter these words is etched in my brain, and I can't help but smile when I think about it! My grandmother was sassy! She had every right to be, for that matter. The things she went through did not dictate her direction. I knew her only as a single woman, and I always admired how she carried herself. It was not what she did; it was how she did it.

When I think about her, I can see her smile. She was a beautiful woman with soft eyes and full lips. Her smile lit up her whole face. It was genuine and sweet. Even when she was chastising us for something we had done wrong, there was going to be a smile! I can distinctly remember her getting on to one of my little cousins. She may have been two years old. My grandmother spanked her legs and continued in the sweetest voice to explain to her why. Afterwards she rubbed her little legs and soothed her. My cousin went from crying to cooing in a matter of minutes. It was how my grandmother did it!

There are so many examples of her using this phrase! Although she was a single woman and we never saw her with a boyfriend or even a friend of the opposite sex, one of our favorite teases for her was to ask about her "boyfriend!" I would never have any evidence to prove one existed, but her comebacks at times seemed to suggest that it was highly possible. I can't say that she was secretive, but she was not one to allow others in her business, so to speak. It was hers, and she handled it well. It wasn't what she did; it was how she did it.

I would learn years later that her marriage to my grandfather was less than perfect. It is understood that most marriages come with their share of hardships, but those "ships" were very "hard" for her. My grandmother outlived my grandfather, and she was even there at his funeral. I never knew her to drop his name, and she never, not in my presence for sure, said anything against him. Even after he was gone, I never heard her mention the things he had done to and against her. That's how she did it.

He was abusive to her in many ways. I heard some horrible stories, but none from her. She accepted what she could not change, and when she was able to make a change in her life, she never looked back. I am sure it took a lot for her to make the decision to get a divorce in that day and age. I am sure it was frowned upon, and she was more than likely ridiculed about it. She lived in a modest house surrounded by her family. I didn't know her to be a battered woman. I didn't know her to be timid or abused. In a time when many women had to stay in an abusive situation, it was how she did it.

Please don't take any of my words to demean my grandfather. He is not the focal point of this story. He was who he was, and at some point, if not forever, she loved him. Her love for him is another example of her understanding it wasn't what she did about even her loving him, it was how she did it and what she was willing to go through to keep from compromising herself. She had a choice to make about whom she loved more, him or her. I am grateful that she chose herself, even though I have no idea what it truly cost her.

I said before that we would tease her about having a boyfriend. My grandmother traveled a lot, visiting her children and their families. I can picture her suitcase now. It seemed that she always had it packed. We would question her about some of those trips being with her boyfriend. Oh, how she would laugh that laugh and smile that smile! She said once that you wouldn't find a man's toothbrush at her house. He would have to respect her as a woman, and if a man wanted her, he would have to make or provide a place for her. Her point was to carry yourself always as woman. It may have been her past experiences or her marriage specifically, but she was bound and determined that she would never be in the position of being treated "less than" again. She explained to us, her granddaughters, that it was not what you did, but how you did it. Above everything you must have respect for yourself and demand that the man does the same as far as respecting you.

Discipline was a major thing for her. She didn't like children acting out and would not put up with their being spoiled. I don't ever remember her spanking me or my siblings. She didn't have to. Her voice was always stern, yet soothing when she disciplined us. She was nothing like our mother! That is another story all together, if you know what I mean. My mother spanked all of us! Raising our children, I tried a mixture of both of their methods. I would like to believe that I did it to their liking and had their blessings.

Sometimes it is hard not to do things the way you want to. There were days as a mayor that I wanted people to know they couldn't push me around. Some days I wanted to throw my hands up and call it a day. There were times when I was disappointed by the people I expected to be on my side, and I wanted them to know it in no uncertain terms. I would be lying if I said I did the right thing every single time. It was important for me to represent my faith and my family well. Many times, even now, people will remark about how I stood through everything that was done to me with style, grace, and class, even though in most cases it was an issue of disrespect and sabotage. My reason and my response are the same: "It's not what you do, but how you do it!"

Chapter Six

You Can't Miss What You Can't Measure

This is a common saying, but I do believe my grandmother said it best. She may have been the first person I knew to say it. Or maybe it just stuck out more with me. The way she said things was almost like a mystery to me. This saying was no different. When I think now about the context in which she used it, I am that much more in awe of her! The lady was truly something else.

I can only imagine what her life was like as a married woman. As before mentioned, I knew her only as a single woman. There had to be some comforts she left behind when she made the decision to leave her husband. What was the final thing, the last straw, the point of no return? What did he do to make her walk away from everything he had provided? She left him in a time that most women stayed because of the kids, the house, no income of their own, no way to start over, nowhere to start, and no man. She obviously stayed longer than she wanted to, but when she could no longer measure the need to stay, there was nothing she would miss.

What do other people really do for us? Why do we put up with certain things when the bad far outweighs the good? We find ourselves in situations in which we have to do some measuring—if only we can. I remember the summer of my senior year in high school. My sister and I were working at Gibson's Department Store as cashiers. We had made plans to take a vacation together and had requested it to be placed on the schedule. For whatever reason, the manager waited until the last minute to refuse it. My sister and I, after a few words with the manager, made the decision to take our vacation as scheduled. Needless to say, the manager did not appreciate the fact that we had gone against his authority. While he did not fire us per se, he removed our names from the schedule. Ultimately, it was the same outcome.

This was a pivotal moment in both our lives. How important was a job that did not respect you enough to appreciate not only your work, but your worth? We were good workers, but we were also not willing to allow our goodness to be taken for weakness. The manager planned to put us in a position where we would have to ask, or even beg, for our jobs back. Taking our names off the schedule and not firing us was his way of making sure we were not eligible for unemployment. To us, he was insinuating that we didn't want to work, or that we had to keep working for his store. Either way, we were not having it! He had no idea with whom he was dealing with at the time. We were Eva's grandchildren! We both walked away from that job to better jobs and better pay! He mistakenly thought we would miss something that we couldn't even measure. That job didn't measure up!

I can recall my grandmother saying the same thing about relationships. She had reached a point in her life by the time I came along that she didn't think wasting your time on something that was not beneficial made sense. I have mentioned how she would share her opinion, which was always fact, concerning my choice of boyfriends. The caution of not wasting your time would be, "you can't miss what you can't measure."

If I am honest, I will have to admit that it never really made sense to me at all when she would say that line. How did the words "miss" and "measure" go together? It puzzled me for a long time, even though I liked the sound of it. I was reminded of a song with the same words in my mind. The truth of the matter is we don't measure things enough. That is how we determine the important things in our lives. It's like counting the cost or measuring the weight. Does it pay? Will it fill up anything? Things that don't do either one has no value. They don't take up enough space or maybe not the right space. It's not enough to count, so it's not enough to miss. When I finally got the meaning and finally understood the concept...another win for my grandmother!

As a mayor, I encountered some relationships that had me fooled early on. Women are considered emotional creatures, but I didn't have the luxury to be led by my emotions. I had to be logical about so many things, including friendships. There were a few people that I realized were merely taking up space in my life. They proved that their worth in my life did not measure up to the point of being significant. I don't mean to sound cruel, but sometimes the truth is not nice. Once I counted the cost and the worth to me was negative, I had to dismiss myself, and I knew they would not be missed. I learned it is not only with people in relationships, but also with things we think we need. I didn't aspire for praise, power, or position. Those things didn't matter to me, so when they were threatened and, in some cases, taken, they didn't make the cut or measure up. And guess what? I didn't even miss them!

We must learn what is important to us. We put value on people and things on which we can't depend. It is up to us to make the determination as to whether they truly make the cut. If you discover those things leave you empty and unfulfilled, you know they don't measure up. You can't measure something that is actually nothing. And you have to admit *nothing* is hard to miss.

Chapter Seven

Let Me Fix You Something To Eat

A few phrases come to mind for this chapter. One is "home is where the heart is," and another is "the way to a man's heart is through his stomach." We would visit my grandmother at least twice a year at her house in Pearl River, LA. It is very close to Slidell, LA, and not too far from New Orleans, LA. We would generally get there at night, since it is about six hours away from El Dorado, AR, where we lived. No matter what time we got there, my grandmother would always say, "Let me fix you something to eat."

My dad was not a big, big man. He had a pretty good-sized stomach, though. I always thought she assumed he would be hungry. Usually, he would have a little something. The later it was for us, the kids, the more we just wanted to go to bed. Her house wasn't very big, and her kitchen was to the left when you walked in. The bathroom was right next to it. She would have on what we would call a "moo moo" and scarf of some type on her hair. These were her "night clothes," because she would have been asleep before we got there. I guess she would be resting so that she would be ready to cook when we got there!

I loved her breakfast! Since we usually were ready to go to bed once we got there, we would be ready for breakfast once we finally got up. I remember eggs (which were not scrambled like my mother's eggs), grits, biscuits, and sausage! I remember the sausage at her house was not like the sausage we had at home. She always had both sausage links and sausage patties, and she didn't cook her sausages the way my mother did either. Her patties were smaller but thicker. The links a different brand, but the way she fried them made them very crispy. I can see her in the kitchen moving around effortlessly in that small space. The smell of breakfast would wake us up, and the aroma would lead us to the table. She would be fixing plates as we entered one by one. She loved to see us eat.

Although she was always expecting us, each time we visited, she would have to go to her favorite grocery store, County Market. My father loved this store! He would joke about going every time. We didn't have a County Market here in El Dorado at the time, so we only knew about the one in Slidell. We never stayed more than a couple of days, because it was always a trip with several stops. Her house was usually the first of many. Even with that knowledge, she still had to get more breakfast food and enough food for several days. My parents had five children, so there were seven of us. My grandmother lived alone, so she definitely had to go beyond her normal grocery bill for us to visit. I guess, in retrospect, it never made sense for her to buy groceries before we got there. I told you my grandmother was smart!

There was also the fact that she didn't drive. She had plenty of people to take her where she wanted to go, but the trip to the grocery store for us was our adventure! She knew where everything was that she needed, and she always let us pick out something we wanted. She and my father would always have an exchange at the register. They both were determined to pay. She never won that argument, but she never lost either. My father would pay one way or the other. He was the best, and although she didn't play favorites, if she had, he would have been it. He knew she would feed him!

We look at food in different ways in our families. I would say culture, but even in each culture there is a difference in each family. My grandmother saw food as nurturing. It was her way of taking care of her family. Preparing a meal for us was love. She loved to do it, not only because we needed it, but because it was her offering to us. She knew the time she took to prepare it would be appreciated when we ate it. I don't know that she loved to cook. I have no idea how long she had been cooking. Considering the time she was born, I would assume most of her life. I do know that she seemed to love to cook for us! She was always happy in that kitchen! Her mood dictated ours. We were happy in her kitchen and loved for her to cook for us!

Those words, "Let me fix you something to eat," still ring in my ears at times. My mother had that same way of nurturing people with food. She seemed to love to cook and watch people eat. They didn't have the same technique, the same stature, or even the same smile. They did have the same way of offering you something to eat that almost always made you respond with a "yes!" In all the years of visiting my grandmother, I can't say that I really remember the two of them cooking together in her kitchen. Maybe it was my grandmother's way of nurturing my mother. She had traveled hours with five small children in the early years. The simple statement was always offered to my mother as well when she said, "Let me fix you something to eat."

I find it funny thinking about it at this moment. She always made the offer. She never anticipated that we would enter her home full. She always considered we would be hungry. Someone always was, for that matter. Food was a tool of kindness, nurturing, and love in my grandmother's arsenal or tool kit. She was equally happy eating good food. She was a full-bodied woman, so you could tell food played a prevalent role in her life. Fixing you something to eat made her happy. My grandmother knew her home was filled with love, and she transferred that love everywhere she went. She was "home" for us, she was our heart. Although she shared herself in so many ways, through our stomachs was one of her favorite ways.

My grandmother's and mother's love for cooking didn't trickle down to me. I don't mind cooking, but I don't have the same skill set that either one of them possessed. I do, like both of them, enjoy watching people enjoy good food, especially if I had a hand in preparing it. I don't have the same food nurturing spirit. I know it is a different era, but I generally expect that people have already eaten when they visit us. If they are invited over for a meal specifically, there is the offer to eat. My husband is the cook in our home now. I wonder how they would feel about that.

Ultimately, I do have a nurturing spirit. As a mayor, I prepared a nurturing plate of "food for thought" for the citizens of this city and anyone else who might need it. When you entered my office, I offered you a seat, and I would serve you with a smile. I took great pride in serving, and my service tool of choice is my ability to speak with wisdom. While food for thought does not enter the stomach, it can be very satisfying to those who receive it. Sometimes it's a healthy meal, the main course, or a hearty snack. I'm grateful for the women in my life who taught me by example to nurture. I hope you have accepted from someone the offer to "fix you something to eat." Chew on the truth!

Chapter Eight

Don't Worry About Me, Baby

My grandmother was an amazing lady! She was resilient, she was nurturing and loving, she was independent, and she was my "she-ro"! I can still hear her voice, her laugh; and I can still feel her spirit. She was never one to have people make a fuss over her. I am not sure whether that spirit of independence was a declaration that she did not need anyone, or whether it was a declaration that she just never wanted to be dependent on anyone again. No matter what the reason may have been, she was a force all on her own.

Instead of needing, she was always assisting. Even to her grown children, she was nurturing.

Something about her spirit meant freedom to me. Her voice sang for me in my dreams long after her transition. Her movements, even as an older woman, were graceful. Although she should have been treated like a queen, she never wanted the attention such treatment would bring. Instead of ever asking for any type of help, when anyone asked her what she needed, her reply usually would be, "Don't worry about me, baby." I loved to hear her say that! I loved what it meant, even when I didn't fully understand. Translation in my mind: "Sweetheart, don't worry your little head about me, because I can take care of myself."

There were so many things about her I wanted to emulate. There were so many ways I wanted to be like her when I was younger. The older I get, the more I want that. Our situations are different for sure. Her past before I knew her is not something I can even imagine, but somehow it didn't damage her love for herself, her children, her family, for life in general.

That's what I wanted; that's what I still aspire to be: Someone who lives life to the fullest!

Independence can sometimes make you better, and not having anyone can put you in the mindset of not needing anyone and of being able to handle things yourself. It can also make you bitter: not having anyone when you need someone can make you feel alone and even left out. My grandmother definitely was not bitter, from my perspective. With her background, though, she had every right to be. She took her past in stride and made her future bright. I loved the affection in her voice whenever she responded, "Don't worry about me, baby."

You can imagine that most of the family wanted to take care of her in some way or another. We loved her presence! Now she wasn't a docile little lady. She never seemed to need assistance. In my mind, I still can see her getting around more like one of my mother's sisters rather than her mother. When we asked if we could do something for her, it was always out of courtesy and tradition instead of actually thinking she needed us to do anything. I think there were times we would ask her only to hear her response, "Don't worry about me, baby."

I so wanted her zest for life! She was known to visit her children in New Orleans on a mission just to walk around and shop the whole day. When she was done, she would head back. Although she had long, beautiful hair, she often wore it in a ball on top of her head. You would think, or at least I did, that she would show it off. To keep from dealing with it, she even wore an array of wigs. Even when it came to getting ready for her day of being out, there was no need to worry about doing her hair. You never knew how it might be when she returned from her day of being out. I can recall at least once being with her. She was very nonchalant about her appearance, but she was always so pretty to me! She didn't command attention, and she didn't require concern.

When she visited us, she just went about her business, being busy around the house with our mother. Some of my mother's friends would always come by to see her. It was as if royalty were in the house. I loved her style. She would wear some of her house dresses that she wore at her house. They may not have been special, but they were different to us at the time. She commanded the room by nature. It was as if we sat at her feet when she spoke. My mother's friends had their favorite lines that she would say. I guess we all did. No matter what she said, her mannerism always spoke, "Don't worry about me, baby."

I don't think I ever really told my grandmother what she meant to me. It is amazing after all this time that the memories of her are so vivid. How I wish there were a memory of all her children and her grandchildren gathered around her expressing how much she meant to us all. I didn't have the pleasure of introducing my daughter to her, but VaShaylia distinctly spoke of her when she was a toddler. I wanted to believe that while the saying is that babies are a gift from God, my grandmother met her in heaven. Maybe she whispered to her that she would be my baby. Maybe she told her to tell me not to worry about her.

This book, although I talked about writing it with other cousins for years, is largely at the urging of my daughter. I pray that this is the chapter that I got right for her. I always wanted to command a room like my grandmother with little to no effort: to speak in a calm voice but have it speak volumes of wisdom loudly. My prayer was to give my daughter and other women an example of a woman that accepted help when help was needed but could also be the assistance that others required at times. I wanted to move in this world as my grandmother did, with grace and not flash. I wanted to have substance that would shine.

My mother had a few favorite sayings that I still use today as well. One that sticks with me in so many situations is, "If you are going to pray, don't worry; and if you are going to worry, don't pray." As a woman of strong faith, I have made the choice to pray. Maybe that is what my grandmother meant in most cases. She understood that she didn't need anyone to fuss over her. Even as an older woman, she didn't require assistance. With a smile on her face, she was telling us she was covered, that God had provided everything she needed. For everything that had happened to her and everything she would go through, there was no need to worry since she was praying her way through!

If I could see her one more time and have one more conversation with her, I would love to tell her that she made one of the biggest impressions on my life by just being herself. Then I could tell her with every accomplishment I have made, she is one of the women that deserves the credit. She raised my mother to be a strong woman, a loving wife, and a doting mother. I could tell her that my daughter loved her through us and thank her for picking her for me, as I pictured it in my mind. Maybe we could share one more embrace before I could kiss her cheek one more time and tell her I love her. She definitely would say she loves me, too! As I walked away, she might say, "Take care of yourself," to which I could reply, "Don't worry about me, baby."

Acknowledgements

It took me a long time to sit down with my thoughts of my grandmother to write this book. I would like to thank my daughter, VaShaylia Brianne Creer, for relentlessly encouraging me to make time and just do it. I am sure my grandmother loves her! I see some of her in my baby.

My mother made sure her children knew her mother in all her strength. I thank her for never tainting our view of her parents. She let us love them both. We didn't blame her father or pity her mother. My mother loved and respected them both and never treated them in a way other than that of a respectful child. Having been one of their oldest children, my siblings and I watched our mother just be their daughter. Their relationship was beautiful despite some of their not-so-appealing past. She proved that she listened to the words her mother said and said some of the most profound things herself.

Although my father was a son-in-law, he loved my grandmother like his own. I loved the way they loved each other. He made sure she always knew she was welcome in our home and assured her that he would always make a way for my mother to come see her. I remember seeing him cry when she transitioned. He was tickled by some of the things she said, but he listened with his ears and his heart.

While my cousins miss her as much as I do, I know we all have our own personal memories of our grandmother. I love the way we get together and recite our favorite ones, especially the ones we share. She will live on in her remaining children Aunt Bessie, Aunt Jessie, Aunt Easter and Uncle Tommie, her grandchildren, and great-grandchildren. We all have a piece of her in our hearts.

I am grateful that my husband not only met my grandmother, but also got her seal of approval. She told me she liked him and that he was the one. My wedding was one of the first that she didn't get to see, although I am sure she was proud on that day. Twenty-seven years later, she was right again! I am thankful that we get to live the prayers she prayed for us.

To everyone that had a hand in helping make this book a reality, I thank you! For every time I was able to pour into someone else's life a wisdom that transcends me in every way, I credit most of it to the lessons learned from "the things my grandmother used to say."